Echoes Of Emotion

A journey through calm waters and fierce fires, shooting stars and dark nights

Sanjam Kaur Saini

BookLeaf Publishing
India | USA | UK

Made with ❤ on the BookLeaf Publishing Platform
www.bookleafpub.in
www.bookleafpub.com

Dedication

I've thought of writing this dedication a million different ways but the one thing that remained constant no matter what was the people I'd be writing it for, my pillars of support. The ones on whom I can count on in both the quiet and the crowd, the sunshine and the storm.

First of all, I'd like to thank God for guiding me through all that I have done in the past 15 years. Every opportunity I'm presented with reminds me just how fortunate I am and that fills me with gratitude each time.

To the ones who have done more for me than I can ever imagine - my dear mom and dad, I know a thank you is never going to be enough but I hope you know how much I appreciate you. To my mother, who filled my childhood years with learning and laughter, always encouraged me to put myself out there and never failed to raise me with love and care, you mean the world to me and I thank you endlessly for always believing in me. Thank you for always being there, through the highs and lows and for supporting me through whatever new project I take on. To my father who's my cornerstone and the one who navigates through tough times with me, the one who who would always get me books when returning from his travels and helped me edit and refine this novel even after long days. Thank you for nurturing each of my interests, for providing opportunities like these and motivating me to make it to the finish line. Thank you for helping me grow, learn and explore under your unending support. Both of you inspire me to work harder each day because that's what you do for me. I learnt to dream big because both of you did it first. You will forever be my greatest inspiration and the values that you have taught me will stay with me forever. From telling my 9 year old self that she should keep writing and that her poems were amazing (even when they weren't) to then guiding me through writing my own novel, your unwavering support is what makes this possible and what gets me through the tough times. Dear mom and dad, thank you, truly.

Dear grandma and grandpa, thank you for standing beside me through it all, for adding so much joy and love into my life and for all the encouragement, always. Dear grandma, your warm hugs, home cooked meals, vivacious stories and big heart shaped my childhood years, added colour to dark times and got me through it all. Thank you for reminding me to keep chasing my goals and for always showing me how much you care. Dear grandpa, thank you for celebrating my achievements and teaching me to learn from my failures.

Thank you for all you do for our family, for sharing your wisdom and always offering the endless love that uplifts me, even when I feel like giving up. Both of you have taught me to aim high by inspiring me with your perseverance, generosity and tenacity. Thank you for making my life so much brighter, helping me jump into new challenges and for the encouragement that made this possible.

To my wondrous, ineffable little sister, thank you for being my partner in crime, my best buddy through it all and the one that adds life and fun in all we do. I don't know what I did to deserve a sister like you but I'm so grateful for the bond we have. No matter what life brings, I know we'll be okay because we'll get through it together. Thank you Sirjan, for teaching me to be carefree and being the one I take on life's journeys with. Your selflessness, vibrant personality, loving nature and shining smile make the world brighter. You're the greatest blessing I could have ever asked for and I want you to know that I will always be there for you, throughout it all. Being your elder sister is a gift that I will cherish for my entire life. Always know that I'm by your side and if you're ever unable to contact me, open this book. I hope that you'll be reminded of me and always remember, there's a poem for you in here that I hope cheers you up on your hardest days. Thank you for the hugs, the conversations and the days that we bake or watch movies or play games together, the ones that never fail to make my heart lighter and mind calmer. I love you so much Sirjan, my little ray of sunlight. I hope you never stop believing in the magic and truly become the queen of Sirjania one day.

A huge shoutout and thank you to the entire Saini family for their constant love and kindness throughout my childhood. Dear family, I truly hope to make you all proud someday.

To all my school teachers and to everyone who has been a teacher or mentor of mine, thank you for all your valuable insights, both the lessons that you taught me inside the classroom as well as out and for never failing to impart your knowledge. My teachers have been an integral part in shaping who I am and have been the role models that taught me how to never give up. I give my forever gratitude and everlasting appreciation to them for always being the guiding light that illuminates the path ahead. Thank you, my dear teachers, for everything you've done for me these past 15 years.

To my friends, for the crazy nights and deep conversations, for the impromptu sleepovers and FaceTime calls at random times. Life wouldn't be the same without my dynamic group of girls that add a touch of magic wherever they go. Thank you for being the ones I can count on, the ones who make me smile bigger than ever and the ones who helped me create some of my most unforgettable memories. I'm so incredibly lucky to have people like you in my life. Thank you for getting me through stressful days and celebrating every milestone with me. I love you all dearly.

To each person who's inspired my poems, know that you play a vital role in my life and contribute more than you can ever imagine. I am so grateful for each and every one of you.

To you, my dear readers, for picking up this book and becoming a part of the family that explores the next few pages. I hope these poems help you feel like you're not alone, that these words make you feel pure emotion. I hope you find a poem to dedicate to your loved ones to show them how much you care or a poem that gets you through tough times. I hope that reading this takes you on an emotional roller coaster as you navigate through the plethora of topics I've penned my thoughts on over the years. I hope this gives you a small glimpse into my life and that some of these resonate with you. Most importantly, I hope you see the power of words and feel inspired to pick up the pen and jot down your thoughts, feelings, worries or ambitions because the main aim of poetry is to self reflect and introspect - something that's becoming increasingly significant in our fast paced world.

Preface

This book is a collection of poetry that attempts to capture a vast variety of different emotions. The book contains messages to the different important people in my life but also messages that I've written to myself over the years. I believe that poetry is one of the best ways to capture feelings and string them into words and that is what I have tried to do throughout this book. From poems I wrote for my family to introspective, self reflecting ones that spawn amidst tough moments or trying times, this book is like a lens into my life and the different aspects or shades of it. After all, life is a challenging, complicated path and throughout the twists and turns, highs and lows, I turn to poetry to be my one constant. From poems that I've worked on for days on end to the ones that sprung like an ignited fire in the middle of the night, all the messy but special thoughts and reflections of mine are encapsulated here. My adolescent years were shaped and characterised by the poems I would fill my google docs with and so I thought it would be a good idea to compile it all into one, cohesive book.

Acknowledgements

To the people who make the good days brighter and the hard days more bearable, this one's for you...

1. Dear Mom,

Dear mom, this poem is specially for you,
For all that you have done and all that you do.
On your special day, I want you to see,
That how much I love you can never be expressed by me.
Thank you for making me who I am today, and
correcting me when I am wrong,
I will be grateful to you all life long.
Thank you for being there and standing by my side,
When I call you my mother, my heart swells with pride.
I hope you know how much you mean to me,
I wish you a very happy birthday, full of glee.
I hope you know that you have an irreplaceable place in
my heart,
Things will change as time goes by, but the bond we
have can never be torn apart.
Thank you for standing next to me and watching me
grow,
How special you are to me, I can't and never will be able
to show.
Dear mother, to me, you're worth more every ruby or

gem,
If I’m a tree, then you’re my stem.
If I’m a bird, then you’re my wings,
If I’m a guitar, then you’re my strings.
If I’m a book, then you’re my pages,
If I’m a poem, then you’re my phrases.

2. Dear Dad,

'Father,' a name I'm so grateful I get to say,
And think about every single day.
A father is a friend, teacher and guide,
And someone whom you can always count on to be by your side.
Thank you for celebrating the good times with me and being there during the bad,
I'm the luckiest and proudest girl in the world as I can call you my dad.
You inspire me every day for you are determined, hardworking and smart,
My life would be incomplete without you, and I love you with all my heart.
Thank you for everything that you have done for me,
How thankful I am to have a dad like you, I hope you see.
You are like the light that brightens up my way,
And no matter where you go, in my heart you will always stay.
Dear Dad, I want to thank you for all you do,

I hope I grow up to be just like you.
You're not just my dad, but also my best friend.
You've stuck by me form the start so I'll stick by you till the end.
How much I love you, it's my turn to show,
How much you mean to me, I hope you know.
Batman is strong, and Superman is too,
But I don't need them as long as I have you

3. Dear grandma and grandpa,

I can't put in words how much you mean to me, I love you so much
Whenever you're around everything seems better, It's like you have a magic touch.
Things will change as the years go past,
But the place you have in my heart will forever last.
Thank you for supporting me throughout my life from the start,
Distance can't ever separate us for you will always be with me, in my heart.
Thank you for standing next to me and watching me grow,
How special you are to me, I can't and never will be able to show.
You add joy and laughter to my mundane days,
Your love and encouragement has shaped me in so many ways.
This precious bond is a true blessing,
Thank you for making life a much more beautiful thing.

You're an amazing person, a true inspiration.
I truly appreciate you so much and look up to you with immense admiration.
May your day be fantastic and as special as you are,
You fill the room with positivity and happiness just like a shooting star.
Thank you, for always being there for me,
To have you, I am really, truly lucky

4. Dear little sister,

Dear sister, I want you to see,
That how much I love you can never be expressed by me.
Dear sister I want you to know,
That how much you mean to me, I can't and never will
be able to show.
I hope you know how special you are in my life, you're
my sister, my supporter, my dearest friend,
I have been walking down the path of life with you from
the start and will still be right next to you till the end.
When you're going through tough times and life turns
upside down,
I'll wipe away your tears and reverse your frown.
When you fall down I'll lift you up,
I'm always there to fill your empty cup.
You'll always have my shoulder to lean on no matter
how old we grow,
I'll always have your back, and cheer you up when
you're feeling low.
Dear Sister, I'm always here for you, I want you to know,
I've held you when you were a baby, and now everyday,

I get to watch you grow.
As you grow older and drive past life, I'll have your back
and be your supporter, every step of the way,
We're not just sisters, we're friends, we're a team, our
bond is super special, and that's how it will stay.

5. For my wonderful teacher,

There is a teacher, extremely special to me,
She is encouraging, kind, the best teacher there can be.
She treats everyone with so much love and care,
I thank her for always being there.
Her beautiful eyes shimmer, and her pretty smile is so radiant,
She is someone I can talk to, her personality is so vibrant.
She is a teacher who I love with all my heart,
A teacher who has been by my side since the start.
A teacher so amazing, she makes my whole day,
A teacher who I'll never forget and in my memories she will always stay.
A teacher who's always supported me, she truly is great,
To have her in my life, I am the most fortunate.

6. Dear teacher,

Dear Ma'am, I dedicate this poem to you,
For all that you have done and all that you do.
For making me who I am today, and correcting me when I am wrong,
I will be grateful to you all life long.
Thank you for supporting me and standing by my side,
When I call you my teacher, my heart swells with pride.
You have taught me how to never give up and how to spread my wings and soar,
You've not just educated me but done so much more.
I truly am grateful to you, from the bottom of my heart,
For standing by my side from the start.
Thank you for being there for me, and expanding my mind,
You are my biggest inspiration, for you are selfless, brave, and kind.
You are an amazing teacher, you always try your best,
To have been a student of yours, I am extremely blessed.

7. To the teachers that shaped my world,

Here’s poem written from the heart,
For a teacher who plays an incredibly vital part.

In halls of learning, you shine so bright,
sparking passion through your insight.

With each lesson, knowledge you bestow,
Planting seeds for our minds to grow.

Through challenges faced, you stand beside,
Instilling courage, erasing doubt's tide.

Through all the classes, I was never, ever bored,
An everlasting impact and several memories you have forged

From funny moments to learning experiences,
Your smile, your classes and your teaching is something I will definitely miss

I know we didn't deserve to have a teacher like you,
but I'm so glad to have been your student, a plethora of chapters you've gotten us through.

You've seen me laugh, you've seen me cry,
As I discovered the world of education, you always stuck by.

You've always been there, an inspiration for me to look up to,
My love for learning has multiplied, all because of you.

I'm going to miss the small moments, that I record in my mind,
Like the classes we spent laughing and how the courage to chase my goals you helped me find.

I'm going to miss the classes, the memories made,
You helped me create the most special moments of this grade.

You've always lead by example and are always there,
you're kind, encouraging, motivating and you always seem to care.

Dear ma'am, you've taught me more than words on a

textbook, in your teaching your passion truly shows,
you left an impact, which I'll never forget, even as this chapter starts to close.

You helped us grow even in the rain,
You poured in sunlight and watered the small bud that came.

You shone the light for us to follow,
You showed us that even if today goes wrong, there's always tomorrow.

You brought me into the world of knowledge and made it eternally fun.
I loved your classes, every single one,

Dear teacher, you're truly adored,
In my memories, you'll be forever stored.

8. To my ride or dies,

I know two girls, the most special in the world,
They have the prettiest eyes and the funniest stories they've told.
They mean the world to me and I'm so incredibly grateful for them,
We became a vibrant trio and a friendship filled with love and support began to stem.

They make me life so much better, their beautiful personalities nothing ever dims,
When we're together, a time of laughter and the creation of fond memories begins.
They're the biggest supporters and nicest companions ever,
Our friendship seems like it will last forever.

They're truly awesome, and here's reason number one,

My favorite season is the summer and they remind me of
the sun.
Their laugh is more melodious than the best music,
And our bond is stronger than a house made of brick.

Hanging out with them is like walking through a field of
flowers in the spring,
so many memories, joy and happiness they bring.
Life's complicated but with the nights of going crazy and
insane conversations, we'll find our way,
Because when I'm with them, it's as perfect as cold
coffee on a warm day.

Their smiles radiate positivity wherever they go,
With them, it's impossible to ever feel low.
Their personalities shine brighter than the stars in the
sky,
They've always been there for me so I won't ever say
goodbye.

Because this friendship is a gift, the most precious one
I've ever gotten,
I know that a life with them will be one filled with
immense fun.
So I really, truly want them to see,
how special they are and how much they mean to me.

No sunset could capture the beauty they hold,
No ocean could match their characters, so vivacious and beautifully bold.
They're a blessing I don't know what I did to deserve,
In my memories, the moments I share with them will be forever preserved.

To my ride or dies, I dedicate this poem to you,
for all that you've done and all that you do.
For adding colour to my life and always making me smile,
my appreciation for you both extends more than the river Nile.

Thank you for sticking by me even when life's challenges unfurled,
You both are more precious than the shiniest diamonds and you deserve the world.

A special place in my heart, our bond holds,
In case you can't tell, I love you

9. Friendship through science...

You're like a coronary artery because you're wrapped
around my heart,
you're like my oppositely charged ion because even high
temperatures can't cause us to part.

If I was an an enzyme, you'd be my optimum
temperature,
If I'm a free electron then you've got good electrical
conductivity for sure.

You're like a specialised cell because you're perfectly
adapted to being the best friend there can be,
My love for you is equal to tan 90 - constantly reaching
infinity.

If you're the North Pole of a magnet then I'm the south,
You're the amino acids and glucose that my cells can't
grow without.

You're as essential to me as magnesium is to leaves,
Our bond is as strong as the double hydrogen one that a
polynucleotide strand can weave.

You're the second part to my homologous chromosome,
if momentum = mass into velocity then together through
life's adventures we'll roam.

Newton said that an object at rest will stay at rest,
Therefore a friendship this special will stay this special
and that theory I'd love to test.

I've seen lots of flame test hues but the most vibrant
thing is your smile,
Life without you would be like a digestive system
without bile.

Pancreas secrete insulin and glucagon but in you I think
they also secrete an "awesomeness" hormone,
When I see you, my circular muscles relax more than
ever because I'm completely mind blown.

Just like lipase turns lipids to fatty acids and glycerol,
you turn mundane days into laughter and fun memories,
The 46 chromosomes in your cells clearly created the
best combination the world can see.

In a 6 mark investigation question about my life, you'd
be an important part, highlighted in the ATP mark
scheme,
My biggest cheerleader, my second half, you've always
been.

I tried out a couple different analogies and similes but
even science can't explain,
How life without you would be like a human without a
brain.

10. Celebration through subjects

Roses are red,
The syllabus is long,
But today's about you,
So nothing can go wrong.

In Chemistry class, reactions explode,
But your smile breaks every periodic code.
You've got more sparkle than any flame test hue,
You + me = a stable molecule.

In Hindi you've written essays and plays,
And tackled tough questions in so many ways.
But no fancy *shabd* can quite express
How much your friendship means to me because even a million words would be too less.

From summaries to the effect created by the writer,
You make even Paper 2 feel lighter.
You're better than any comprehension clue,

And your story arcs? Always something new.

While assets = equity + liabilities,
You = joy + unmatched abilities.
Forget the trial balance, just for a bit,
You're my best friend and that's a solid credit!

We've calculated angles, solved every plot,
But your birthday's the highlight on every dot.
From Pythagoras to Trigonometry, we've been through the grind,
Forget x and y - you're the greatest value I could ever find.

Your neurons might synapse under stress,
But Biology says: you're built for success.
Your heart beats faster, enzymes work hard - exam or cake?
But your birthday's here, so take a break!

Physics laws may try to weigh,
But not even gravity can stand in your way.
You're a force, Newton would agree,
Accelerating into greatness at he highest velocity.

We've had sleepovers wild and wonderfully weird,
Jam sessions loud, and conversations that steered

From memes to dreams to songs at 2AM,
Life's better with you, the person who shines brighter than the world's most radiant gem.

And let's not forget our psychic power,
Manifesting narrative topics at the perfect hour.
Best friend telepathy? Clearly it's real,
This precious bond nothing can ever steal.

You're 15! Wow, who knows what life has in store,
I hope it brings you joy and fulfillment and so much more.
In being the best friend ever, you already have an A*,
I'm so proud of you - you've come so far.

So here's a wish for a brilliant bean,
Whose brain's a certified studying machine.
May your marks be high, your worries low,
And your happiness exponentially grow!

You'll crush these exams, we both know it's true,
But first, happy birthday! The world's a better place because of you.

11. New beginnings...

As another year passes by, we start another chapter in the book,
It's been an incredible journey, we can't go back but we can look.

I had experiences of a lifetime and memories were made,
So much to remember and take away as we finish this grade.

I learned so much this year from English to Science to Math,
But there's so much more to learn as we walk ahead on this path.

This year was filled with amazing times with teachers and friends,
And it is kind of sad to realize that this year has come to an end.

But there's a whole new year we're heading towards and

yesterday's gone,
I can't wait to see what the future holds and it's time to tackle it head on.

With the new academic year comes new goals, a new opportunity,
A chance to acquire more knowledge, a fresh start for you and me.

I am so grateful to everyone that made this year so amazing,
Who knows what the coming year will bring?

12. Human without Humanity?

What destruction was caused by the world war if you
want to know,
you'll have to turn the pages of history and go back to
around 80 years ago.

To a time that was one of the darkest for mankind,
A time where chaos and mayhem is all you'll find.

We say that we want to make the world a better place,
but from economic downfall to the loss of innocent lives,
war has scarred the human race.

Every country stood divided, instead of united, each
nation was prepared with weapons, ready to fight,
It's a shame to think that we cared more about profit and
economy than we did about doing what's right.

From waging wars and failing governments, the effects
of world war 2 still haunt us, even in today's generation,

because even today, We live in a world of destruction, a world where issues are resolved not with words but with a gun.

Countries cared less about their citizens and more about their trade,
Global peace was non-existent, inflation was rising, weapons were everywhere, what a mess we'd made.

So if you ask me the effects of world war 2 are, well, here's my answer,
There are millions of refugees, people live in the fear of getting bombed and there's more wars than there ever were.

We call ourselves human but in world war 2, we lost our humanity,
What a horrible time it was, no amount of facts can help us see.

If only we could get humanity to stay,
maybe we wouldn't face the effect of world war 2, even today,

Humans are the smartest species they say and yet we live in a world of torture, bloodshed, war, conflict and so much more,

Humans are the smartest species they say, well, about that I'm just not so sure.

13. Evolution

We say that we want to make the world a better place,
but from global warming to corruption, we're simply
destroying the human race.

In our world, it's become every nation for itself, each
country's ready to fight,
We now care more about profit and economy than we do
about doing what's right.

waging wars and failing governments, what are we
passing on to our future generation?
I think we're forgetting that positively contributing to
society is the true purpose of education.

Countries care less about their citizens and more about
their trade,
species are extinct, pollution is everywhere, trees are
being cut, what a mess we've made.

We live in a word of poverty and hunger, a world of

destruction,
a world where countries battle as if no damage is being done.

Industries, scientific development and employment rates might be increasing,
but in the name of evolution and progress, so much horror we bring.

Technology is advancing faster than ever, but compassion is left behind,
People who truly care about our society have become so hard to find.

I think it's time to retrace our steps and turn the pages of history,
To find out where we left our empathy.

If only we could go back in time and get it back, what changes it would bring,
evolution, it's such an extraordinarily funny thing.

14.

We say that we want to make the world a better place,
but from global warming to corruption, we're simply
destroying the human race.

In our world, it's become every nation for itself, each
country's ready to fight,
We now care more about profit and economy than we do
about doing what's right.

waging wars and failing governments, what are we
passing on to our future generation?
I think we're forgetting that positively contributing to
society is the true purpose of education.

Countries care less about their citizens and more about
their trade,
species are extinct, pollution is everywhere, trees are
being cut, what a mess we've made.

We live in a word of poverty and hunger, a world of

destruction,
a world where countries battle as if no damage is being done.

Industries, scientific development and employment rates might be increasing,
but in the name of evolution and progress, so much horror we bring.

Technology is advancing faster than ever, but compassion is left behind,
People who truly care about our society have become so hard to find.

I think it's time to retrace our steps and turn the pages of history,
To find out where we left our empathy.

If only we could go back in time and get it back, what changes it would bring,
evolution, it's such an extraordinarily funny thing.

15. Nature from the eyes of an 11 year old...

A magical wonderland where nature blossoms, blooms and more,
Filled with magnificent flora and fauna, it has so much in store.

A place where nature grows and thrives,
With carefully integrated ecosystems, home to so many lives.

A glorious habitat, one we're destroying.
Have we forgotten what nature can bring?

It's habitats like these that keep our world alive,
To preserve, replenish and protect it, we must strive.

To sustain our planet is the responsibility of you and me,
Is the damage we're doing to our environment something we fail to see?

There is more to life than status and revenue, we must
open our eyes,
As society progressed we forgot the significance of
nature in our lives.

It's time to take action before it's too late,
Only when we sustain our habitats will humans truly be
great.

16. She's...

She's everywhere, she's significant, yet someone we don't notice,
Try to guess who she is, first clue, she's moody but undisturbed and full of bliss.

She's terrifying and dangerous when she needs to be,
But she's also calm and relaxing, her view can set you free.

She's destructive and powerful, she has a mind of her own,
Yet she shows more serenity and peace than anyone has ever shown.

A terror when she's enraged, a dangerous force that no one can repel,
At the same time, she knows how to stay composed and collected really well.

No one can stop her, no one can get in her way, not you,

not me,
But she's also unaffected by the world, lives on with
peace and calmness and is the sign of stability.

She's chaos, she's a wonder, she's quiet yet loud, she's
bold yet soft, she's magic,
She can be a friend or a foe, she can be petrifying yet
soothingly serene, no one knows her secret trick.

Full of tranquility, she's a beautiful hue of blue,
She's home to endless life, an ecosystem of her own,
she's a home, that's a pretty big clue.

She's graceful and elegant, a beautiful sight to see,
She's waves, water, the ocean, her character an
inspiration to you and me

17. Who is she?

There was once a girl, a mysteriously peculiar thing,
so many twists and turns she would bring.

She would make us fight endless challenges that only
seemed to grow,
Getting through her is a battle through endless snow.

From early mornings to sleepless nights,
She teaches us how to climb mountains and survive the
toughest fights.

She teaches us the value of hardwork and how to deal
with stress,
Some moments, she makes perfect sense while others,
she feels like a mess.

There are times when she's filled with color and some
where she feels dull,
She's unpredictable and never goes by plan, but that's
what makes her special.

She goes by with the blink of an eye,
She can make you laugh and at times make you cry.

she brings us numerous obstacles but also unending happiness,
she's filled with memories, lessons and journeys, who is she? Can you guess?

She's like a roller coaster ride, filled with ups and downs,
some triumphant moments and some filled with frowns.

Some days good, some bad,
Some memories are joyful, while others sad.

She's life, an unsolved puzzle, the path we all take,
filled with diversions, depending on the choices we make.

She's the most precious gift one could ever get,
use her wisely, or you'll be filled with regret.

As each puzzle gets put into place, so much pleasure it will bring,
Life, it's such a beautiful yet challenging thing.

18. Miss or hit?

She's making a change, it could go either way,
For everything to work out, she'll hope and pray.

New challenges to be faced, new things to learn,
with all the hard work, there's so much to earn.

A huge risk to take, but also a new adventure,
Nervous, scared, worried but excited, that's for sure.

To start this journey, she honestly can't wait,
but she's afraid that to make this change, she's a bit too late.

She spends hours wondering what the outcome will be,
But the learning and experience she'll get from this transition, she's ecstatically looking forward to see.

They say she's burdening herself, that its the wrong path to take,
She's thought so too but at the end of the day, she knows

it's a change she really wants to make.

Will she succeed, will she fail? She’s dying to know,
will it all work out? Only time will show.

She’s worried about her future, but knows that its in her hand,
Who knows in a few months where she’ll land.

All she knows is that she wants to do this and is ready to commit,
it’ll be hard but let’s see whether it’ll be a miss or a hit.

19. Maybe

Maybe I'll fail, I'll mess it up, I'll freeze,
Maybe when I look at the exam paper, my stress will cause any sense of logic will cease.

Maybe I won't understand anything,
Maybe failure and disappointment is all that I'll bring.

Maybe my answers will be horrible, I'll run out of time,
And my anxiousness will only worsen as the clock continues to chime.

But Maybe, just maybe, everything will be just fine,
Maybe, after working so hard, a dream come true will be mine.

Maybe I can pull this off, maybe it's not so bad,
Maybe the world doesn't always have to be gloomy and sad.

Maybe I got this, maybe I don't have to worry day and

night,
Maybe my goal will transition from a vision to a real, beautiful sight.

Because yes, flowers die and hurricanes crash once lively fields,
But flowers also bloom and nature thrives, resulting in spectacular yields.

Yes, ships sink and thunderstorms kill,
Yes, the water's current is throwing me off course but maybe, I'll survive if I believe I will.

Yes, species go extinct and the world is filled with suffering,
But one thing to remember is the resilience of life, it's such a wonderful thing.

So just like an orchid trapped in bad weather,
Just like a lost cub searching for shelter,

I'll stay hopeful because every storm subsides and the sun always rises,
After endless hard work, i'll keep believing that life will reward me with one of its prizes.

Maybe I'll let everyone down, but maybe i'll make them

proud,
Either way, I'm not giving up because to that I've vowed.

After years of doubting, never feeling good enough and thinking of the worst,
I'm finally going to start having faith in myself, because
Maybe, it'll all work out and the world is blessed, not cursed.

Maybe things won't work out but you know what?
Maybe they will,
Because my readiness to keep working is something no failure can ever kill.

20. A to B then why not B to A?

If steam can turn into water then water can turn into steam,
If you can dream of a reality then reality can become that dream.

If fire can come from heat then heat can come from fire,
If you can get a working wire from electric current then you can get electric current from a working wire.

The law of inverse transformation, an interesting one to try,
They used to say "think positive", "believe in yourself" and I used to wonder why.

But our mindset is crucial and our thoughts shape our life, that's important to understand.
Because If a circumstance can produce a psychological state then a psychological state can produce a circumstance

So you can if you believe because you believe you can,
So remember that if you plan for success then success is part of that plan.

If sound can create vibrations then vibrations can create sound,
The effect our state of mind has on our reality is indeed profound.

A situation can change a belief just as a belief can change a situation,
The law of inverse attraction, one that's left me filled with utter captivation.

If you get a plant from a seed then you get a seed from a plant,
What you think holds value, so don't ever say that you can't.

Alter the mind first, then the result will come running,
the law of inverse attraction, isn't it truly fascinating?

21. Why?

I tell my sister I'm proud of her and that I love her, every night,
It's obvious how precious she is, it's embedded in plain sight.

I tell my mother that I admire how hard she works because she really does,
She's so talented, my inspiration she will be, is and always was.

I tell my best friends how amazing they are and how lucky I am to have found my companions,
They're smart and pretty and fun beyond measure, their beautiful personalities nothing ever dims.

I tell my teachers how kind they are and how much they mean to me,
Their intellect and helpful nature, it doesn't take a genius to see.

I tell everyone around me how special they are because I truly believe it,
I'll always notice the good in people, from their persona to their wit.

I'll always try to be a nice person, never step out of line,
But why can I notice everyone else's worth and not mine?

If I spoke to my friends like I did to myself, I don't think I'd have any,
Everyone around me seems perfect in my eyes but when I count my own flaws, there's so many.

I'd never do that to my mother, she doesn't deserve it,
but how do I convince myself that neither do I?
I can't get myself to believe that without the trophies and straight As, I'm still worth something, no matter how hard I try.

Why do I stress myself out and make myself feel like a failure?
Even when I know that I wouldn't wish that upon anyone else, that's for sure.

It's so easy to be nice to everyone else and notice their strengths, it's so easy to love, compliment and help them

all,
Couldn't ever imagine being mean to them and stopping them from standing tall.

So why do I do it to myself? Why do I see a bad grade and immediately feel useless?
When I know that if it were my sister, I'd still view her as nothing short of a princess.

I'd tell her that her report card doesn't define her but when it's mine I think it does,
I'd resent myself for messing up but if it's my sister I'd treat her to ice cream or something else she loves.

Why do I reserve the criticism for me?
As someone who sees the best in everyone, why's the best in me so hard to see?

22. Warning

If I came with a warning what would it say?
If I came with a warning would you read it and shake
your head in dismay?

Warning : cries too easily
Too hard on herself she'll always be.

Warning : pressurises herself a little too much,
Stresses out a lot, from breakfast to lunch.

Warning : obsessed with books to the point it's crazy
Feels like a failure when she let's herself be lazy.

Warning : has dreams too ambitious for her own good,
Won't let herself relax even when she knows she
probably should.

Warning : she cares, she cares a lot but maybe that's not
such a bad thing,
Hardwork, dedication, kindness, empathy, whatever you

want she'll bring.

Warning : never breaks the rules, always does as she's told,
Sets a new goal to accomplish every time life's new challenges unfold.

Warning : hates herself today
because she hates the way stuck in her head she'll always stay.

Warning : never in the present moment, either worrying about the past or planning the future,
prioritises everything except what's best for her.

But sometimes it's good to walk past those warning signs,
Because maybe that's how everything aligns.

23. One day... (for the overthinkers)

Something is always on my chest,
A weight, a burden, anxiousness before a test.

And it never leaves me alone, it's always on my mind,
It makes it impossible to relax and unwind.

The voice in my head is getting too loud,
I stress out too much and of that, I'm not proud.

It keeps telling me I'm not good enough and I've started thinking it's right,
Because I feel like getting through each day is an overthinking filled fight.

I wish it would leave me but it's in everything I see,
In every to do list, every expectation and every perfect fictional character I feel I need to be.

I hate myself today, that actually happens quite often,

Everyday is an overthinking battle with myself, one
which I can never win.

I wish I was smarter, worked harder, studied more, did
better in school,
I try to be the nicest person to the rest of the world, but
to myself I'm so cruel.

And I could try to ignore it, but it's all I think about,
It's like the thoughts in my head want to scream and
shout.

But maybe one day, I'll love myself as much as I love
everyone around me,
Maybe one day, how special I am, I'll finally see

24. Happiness

Happiness is your favorite meal after a long, hard day,
Happiness is having faith in yourself even when you feel like you've lost the way.

Happiness is watching the rainbow flourish after a storm,
Happiness is hot chocolate on winter mornings and a loving family to keep you warm.

Happiness is lending someone a hand and making someone smile,
Happiness is finding friends and hobbies that make this time on earth worthwhile.

Happiness is a beautiful sunset on the beach,
Happiness is achieving the goal that felt out of reach.

What is happiness? The terrifying thing is, it's up to you and me

What is happiness? The exciting thing is, it's up to you and me.

25. 15 years ago..

15 years ago, a girl was gifted with the best parents in the world,
And because of them, she knows she'll be okay no matter what chaos will be unfurled.

Because of them she grew up in a home filled with laughter, movies, books, love and music,
Her childhood was filled with unforgettable memories and support as strong as a brick.

From always being there to being the reason she smiles,
They're the reason she won't ever give up and they make her life worthwhile.

They taught her all she knows, they showed her how to dream big and chase them with all her heart,
They showed her the way and nurtured every interest of hers from the start.

They let her ask every irrational question and be their

little shadow,
They let her explore it all and gave her all she needed to grow.

They gave her faith, they made her feel loved, always,
They're the people she can turn to, they gave her the strength to navigate life's confusing maze.

Because of them, she's the girl she is and she doesn't know what she did to deserve them,
She still has a long way to go but she knows she'll be alright, because to her plant, they're the stem.

Dear mom and dad, I love you more than you could imagine, I hope you know,
How grateful I am not even a million poems in a thousand different languages could show.

15 years ago, a girl was gifted with the best parents in the world,
And because of them, she knows she'll be okay no matter what chaos will be unfurled.

26. I want...

I want warm hugs and reassurement through tough
times,
I want a family to enjoy life with, as if we're a team,
bound together by vines.

I want to promise someone the world and be the one to
give it to them,
I want to be someone's biggest supporter, because every
plant needs a stem.

I want to be the light during someone's dark day,
Life's too short to not experience it all, and the role of a
successful surgeon but also caring person I want to play.

Yes, report cards, trophies and degrees are great, but the
true achievement is being a person who's kind,
I don't just want to be respected, I want to be the reason
someone laughs and feels okay even when life's
challenges unwind.

Because life’s greatest joys come from watching
someone you love smile,
I want to tell my friends that my love for them extends
further than the river Nile.

I want to be the home someone else comes back to,
I want to find and create bonds that are strong and true.

In my time on this earth, I want to love, because I've got
so much of it to give,
A life filled with memories, a life painted by love, that's
the life I want to live.

27. The joy of writing

The joy of writing, one so pleasant and rewarding,
A world of words, a hobby I love, it's truly the best thing.

From poetry to prose, there's a thought behind each line,
Indulging in writing, a favorite pass-time of mine.

A picture painted with words, it unlocks so much imagination and creativity,
Expressing yourself in perfect rhymes, something very significant to me.

Writing has helped me learn the power of words,
How a few lines put together, can make so many feelings heard.

Writing can express emotions of every color or shade,
My passion for it is something that will never fade.

Writing is truly magical, it's become a part of me,

Something truly special in my life, it will always be.

From structured poems to story arcs that go wild,
Writing can both leave you in tears and unleash your inner child.

A world of colours and words spinning around,
Each syllabus carefully woven, like pairing notes to create a melodious sound.

Where words become portals to feelings not shown,
The beauty of language and the comfort of writing is my constant cornerstone.

Writing created rhythm as words flow and calms a roaring sea,
Writing brings people together and can tame any fire ignited in me.

From literature essays to narratives, it's a part of the exams that define my report card,
But more importantly, it's a part of culture and it's part of my heart.

Writing is something I love, something I always look forward to,

It is something I'll never give up because the true joy of writing is sharing it with you.